I dedicate this book to my family, some of whom live their life's impacted by health conditions, many of those described in this book, and to those that have always been there for me and supported me on my own personal journey with Epilepsy and Tourette's Syndrome.

Courtney Wilson © 2023

My Disability and Me

Courtney Wilson © 2023

Hello!

My name is Mya and with the help of my best friends, I would like to teach you all about the different types of disabilities and conditions that affect many children and adults around the world.

It's important to remember that not all of my friends disabilities' are visible, but just because you can't see them, doesn't mean they aren't there.

Understanding someone's disability or condition is important because when you understand, it is easier to be kind.

And we should always be kind to one another.

Hi! I'm Abby and I have Autism

What is Autism?

Well, Autism can happen when someone's brain hasn't developed in the same way as others.

Having Autism means it's a bit harder for me to understand the world around me, and I need a little bit of extra help when it comes to learning and understanding.

Some people with Autism, struggle to talk and even eat. It can also make it harder to make friends, deal with changes and deal with loud noises and bright lights.

It's also harder to detect in girls than boys.

But even though it can be hard sometimes, I know that I'm awesome and my Autism will never stop me!

Hi! I'm Adam and I'm an Amputee

What does it mean to be an Amputee?

An Amputee is someone who has had an **amputation** surgery.

This is when a specialist doctor operates, removing some of or all of a **limb** (arm or leg) or even a hand or foot, due to a serious injury, infection or illness.

It's also important to know that there are other reasons that someone might not have an arm, leg, hand or foot.

It isn't always because of an amputation operation.

Sometimes, a baby's arms, leg, hands and feet, might struggle to develop completely or even at all, so when they are born, they may be missing a limb or have hands and feet that don't quite look the same as many others.

Hi! I'm Asha and I have Alopecia

What is Alopecia?

Well Alopecia is a condition that causes hair loss. This is because my **immune system** (the body's germ fighting team) gets confused and thinks my **hair follicles** (the tiny tunnels our hair grows out of) are bad germs and tries to get rid of them to keep me healthy, but this confusion leads to hair loss instead.

There are different kinds of Alopecia and not everyone goes completely bald like me. But being bald does mean I get to wear really cool wigs!

Hi! I'm Bobby and I'm Blind

What does it mean to be Blind?

Well, being Blind means that I can't see. But this doesn't mean I live in total darkness. Often, people who are Blind can still see a little light or shadows. And there are different reasons someone could be Blind. They could be born Blind just like me, or they may lose or have worse eyesight as they get older.

Like many other Blind people, I have a dog (called Max!) that has been trained to act as my eyes to keep me safe.

However, there are also special canes that Blind people can use instead.

And did you know that people who are Blind can still enjoy books! This is because of something called Braille; where letters and numbers are represented by raised dots on pages, that people who are Blind feel with their fingertips. So I can enjoy books just like the rest of my friends.

This is the Braille alphabet.

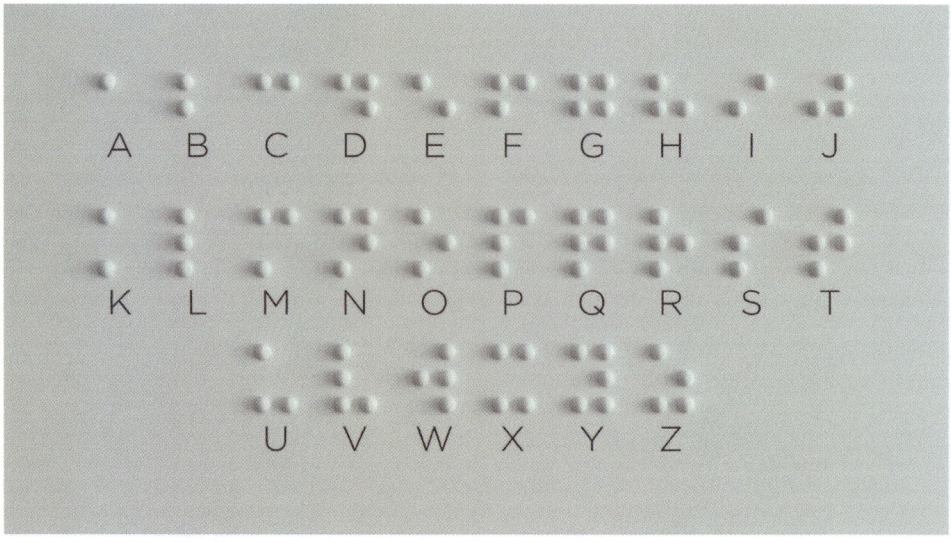

Braille isn't just used in books. It can be found in all kinds of places.

You can also find braille on bus and train travel signs, restaurant menus, food labels, drink labels and even your bottle of shampoo. You can also find braille on the number keypad in a lift, or the keyboard of a computer or laptop.

Even places like museums use braille signs, so blind people can still learn and enjoy.

And, did you know that those bumps on the pavement by road crossings are there to help people just like me. It is called **tactile paving** or **braille paving** and is used to let Blind people, like me, know where to cross and where the end of the pavement is, so they can cross the road safely.

So clever!

Hi! I'm Charlie and I have Cerebral Palsy

What is Cerebral Palsy?

Cerebral Palsy (or CP) affects my whole body. This is because it affects the way my brain talks to my muscles. Because of this I have trouble controlling how my muscles move so I use a wheelchair or frame to help me get around.

Me and many others with CP, also have trouble with our speech. Sometimes what we want to say is unclear, so it takes us just a little bit longer to say what we want to. And when it comes to eating, I also take a bit longer than others, as I need some extra help to do so.

But even though these things take me a little bit longer to do, I will never let my CP stop me!

> Hi! I'm Callie and I have Coeliac Disease

What is Coeliac Disease?

Coeliac Disease is an autoimmune disease. This means that if I or anyone else with Coeliac Disease eats something called **gluten** our **immune system**, will start to fight itself, damaging our **villi (vil-eye)** which is found in the **small intestine**, making us feel unwell.

What do all those terms mean?
- **Gluten** is a protein found in Barley, Rye, Oats, Wheat and Spelt (B.R.OW.S)
- **The Immune System** is the body's germ fighting team.
- **The Small Intestine** is part of the body's digestive system and is lined with Villi.
- **Villi (vil-eye)** help with the digestion of food and help absorb nutrients from the food we eat.

This doesn't stop us from eating lots of yummy foods (I really love cake!). We just have to eat special versions that don't have any gluten in.

Hi! I'm Danny and I'm Deaf

What does it mean to be Deaf?

When someone is Deaf it means their ears don't work in the same way as others.

People can be Deaf for many reasons. Like me, some people are born Deaf or with hearing difficulties and other people may lose their hearing or find it harder to hear if they become sick or as they get older.

Many people with hearing difficulties will use an hearing aid. This is something that goes in the ear and makes things louder so that they can hear better.

People who are Deaf or have hearing problems will also use something called sign language to communicate. This is when they use their hands to make shapes that mean certain letters or words.

Using my Sign Language chart, can you sign your name?

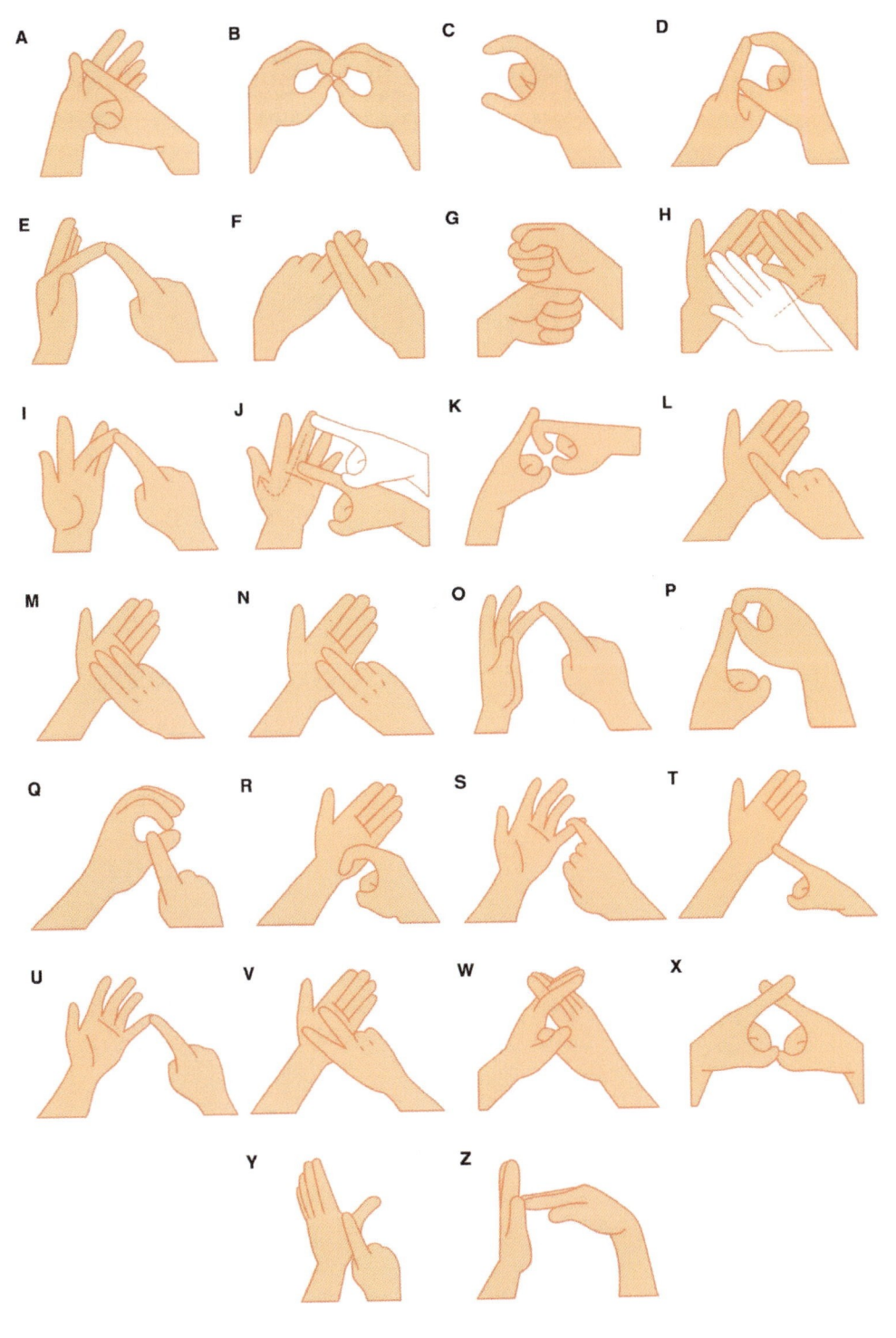

Hi! I'm Darcey and I have Down's Syndrome

What is Down's Syndrome?

Down's Syndrome is a **genetic** condition that affects a baby's brain and body as it develops before being born.

What causes Down's Syndrome?
Well, the body has many different building blocks that come together to make us who we are. One of those building blocks are **chromosomes**. These are string like structures that contain something called **genes**. Genes are the body's decision makers before a baby is born. They decide whether you're a girl or boy, what colour your hair will be, what eye colour you'll have and much more.

Everyone should have **23 pairs** of chromosomes. You get half from your mum and half from your dad. That's **46 in total**. But when someone has Down' Syndrome it is because they have **47** chromosomes in total. This extra chromosome causes the body's building blocks to shift when the baby is developing, which means that baby will be born with Down's Syndrome.

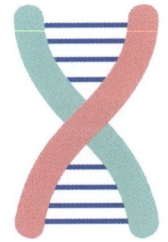

> Hi! I'm Dion and I have Dwarfism

What does it mean to have Dwarfism?

Having Dwarfism means that I am a lot shorter than most people and I walk slightly differently. This is because my bones didn't grow and develop properly before I was born.

The most obvious sign of Dwarfism, is our short stature, often only growing to be 4 feet, 10 inches tall.

Having dwarfism can also cause things like,
- Slow growth
- Difficult mobility
- Heart problems
- Hunched back (sometimes causing back pain)

But even with all of this, most people with Dwarfism (also known as little people), can live pretty normal lives, doing exactly what everyone else can, just with some adaptations. Like having things put lower down, using stools or having a grabbing tool.

Hi! I'm Dexter and I have Type 1 Diabetes

So what is Diabetes?

Well Diabetes is a condition that affects the way the body uses **glucose**; a sugar that helps fuel the body.
Usually, after you eat something, the glucose from your food goes into your bloodstream. Then something called the **pancreas**, makes something called **insulin**, which helps the glucose get to the body's cells, giving it the energy it needs. However for someone with Diabetes, this isn't the case.

I have Type 1 Diabetes. This means my pancreas doesn't produce the insulin I need. My body still takes the glucose from my food, but it can't get to my blood cells, where it's needed. Because the glucose stays in the blood, my blood sugar levels get quite high, which can make me feel unwell.

No one really knows what causes Type 1 Diabetes, but it can be controlled by taking insulin through an **omnipod** like I do, or by using an **insulin pen**.

Then there's something called Type 2 Diabetes. This is different to Type 1, because the body does make insulin in the pancreas, it just doesn't work the way that it should, causing blood sugar levels to get too high. People with type 2 Diabetes don't need omnipods or insulin pens, to help control their blood sugar levels, they do this by eating a healthy and balanced diet.

Hi! I'm Eric and I have Epilepsy

What is Epilepsy?

Epilepsy is something that affects the brain.

We all have a powerful brain that controls everything our body does by sending messages to every part of the body, but if someone has epilepsy, their brain can cause **seizures** (also known as fits, and funny turns) when too many messages are sent.

There are lots of different kinds of seizures and they don't all look the same. For example, an absence seizure just looks like a person with Epilepsy is daydreaming. Others can just be random, uncontrolled arm and leg movements, or sometimes a person with Epilepsy ends up shaking on the floor.

Luckily, there are special medicines that help me and others with Epilepsy control our seizures so we can live wonderful lives, and achieve amazing things.

Hi! I'm Luke and I have Learning Difficulties

What are Learning Difficulties?

Learning Difficulties are conditions that affect the way someone learns and takes in information.

First there's **Dyslexia** (diss-lex-ee-a). If someone has Dyslexia, it means they would struggle with reading, writing and spelling. Things can become a bit muddled up. Another Learning Difficulty that can make writing letters and spelling difficult is **Dysgraphia** (diss-GRAFF-ee-uh).

Then there's **Dyscalculia** (diss-cal-KYOO-lee-uh). This is when someone struggles with maths.

There is also something called **ADHD** (Attention Deficit Hyperactivity Disorder). This is my learning difficulty.

Having ADHD means that I find it harder to sit still, stay focused and pay attention. It also affects my self control. This means that sometimes I can be slightly naughty even when I don't mean to be. But I always try my hardest to be kind to everyone around me.

People with Learning Difficulties may need some more help with learning and staying focused, but we can all still lead happy lives and do amazing things.

Hi! I'm Tessa and I have Tourette's Syndrome

What is Tourette's Syndrome?

Tourette's Syndrome is a condition that affects someone's **central nervous system** (this controls and coordinates the body) causing something called **tics**.

There are two different types of tics; **motor** and **vocal**. Motor tics are movements that we can't control like head shaking, rapid blinking and sudden movement of our arms and legs, and vocal tics are noises we can't control. For example, whistling, tongue clicking and repeating words.

Tics can be so different from person to person, but there is one factor that affects all tics... EMOTIONS.

In fact the song 'If you're happy and you know it, clap your hands' helps define how emotions affect Tourette's in a simple way. If someone with Tourette's feels an extreme emotion, like high levels of excitement or stress, their tics can get worse for a short amount of time. But tics can also calm down when concentrating or relaxing.

Like me, people with Tourette's Syndrome can still live a happy day to day life. Although tics can be hard to manage sometimes, they don't have to hold us back.

I hope my friends have helped you to understand a bit more about disabilities and health conditions.

It's important that we understand what other people are going through and what their disabilities mean, because understanding is the key to being kind. And we should always be kind.

Special Terms to Remember

- **Limbs** - your arms and legs.
- **Chromosomes** - String like structures that contain genes.
- **Genes** - The body's decision makers before we're born.
- **Nervous System** - Controls and coordinates the body.
- **Small Intestine** - Part of the 'digestive system' It helps process the food we eat.
- **Villi - (Vil-eye)**, line the small intestine and help the body digest food and absorb nutrients.
- **Glucose** - Sugars that help fuel the body
- **Pancreas** - Produces insulin
- **Insulin** - Helps the glucose get to the cells.
- **Immune System** - The body's germ fighting team.
- **Hair Follicles** - The tiny tunnels our hair grows out of.
- **Tactile Paving (Braille Paving)** - Bumps on the pavement, telling those who are blind where the pavement ends so they can cross the road safely.

Courtney Wilson

Resources:
kids.britannica.com
achildrenshouse.org
www,merakilane.com
kidshealth.org
www.epilepsy.org.uk
www.cerebralpalsy.org
understandingdwarfism.org

Illustrations: Freepik / Canva / Adobe Stock

Courtney Wilson © 2023

Printed in Great Britain
by Amazon